T0046685

The Wild Cats Book

Rebecca Silverstein

Brought to you by the editors of

My Weekly Reader

Children's Press®
An imprint of Scholastic Inc.

How to Read This Book

This book is for kids and grown-ups to read together—side by side!

A 😊 means it is the kid's turn to read.

A grown-up can read the rest.

Simple text for kids who are learning to read

Harder text—which builds knowledge and vocabulary— for grown-ups to read aloud

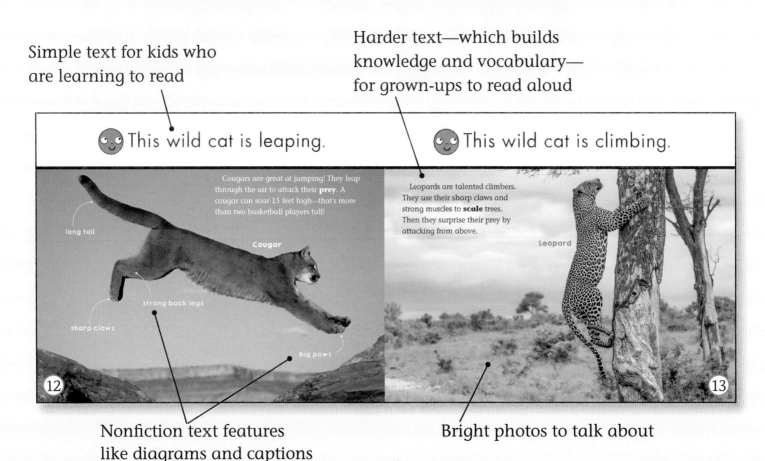

😊 This wild cat is leaping.

Cougars are great at jumping! They leap through the air to attack their **prey**. A cougar can soar 15 feet high—that's more than two basketball players tall!

long tail

Cougar

sharp claws

strong back legs

big paws

😊 This wild cat is climbing.

Leopards are talented climbers. They use their sharp claws and strong muscles to **scale** trees. Then they surprise their prey by attacking from above.

Leopard

12

13

Nonfiction text features like diagrams and captions

Bright photos to talk about

2

Table of Contents

Lion Cub

Tiger

Lion

Chapter 1

World of Wild Cats

There are about 40 kinds of wild cats. Let's meet some of them!

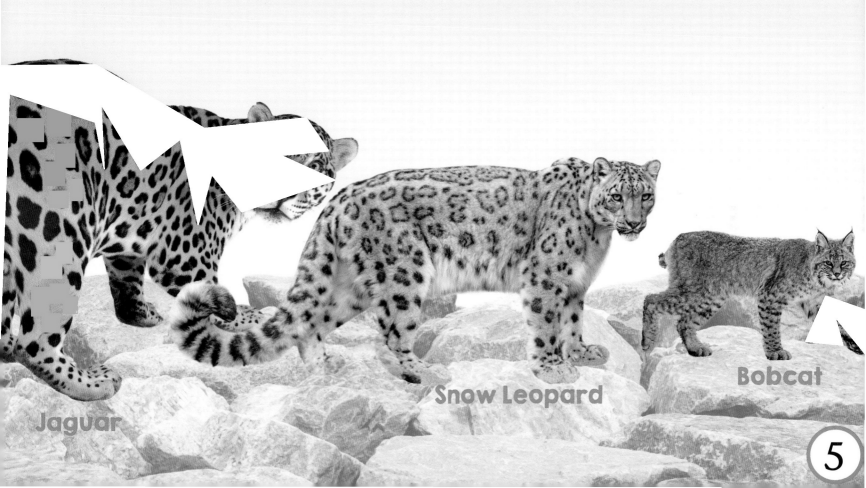

Jaguar

Snow Leopard

Bobcat

This is a lion.

Lioness

Cub

Lion

Meet the lion, the king of the beasts! Most wild cats live alone, but lions live in a **pride**. A male lion has a **mane**, but a lioness does not.

mane

This is a tiger.

Tigers are some of the biggest wild cats.
Like all wild cats, tigers are **carnivores**.
A tiger can eat 90 pounds of meat in one meal.
That would make about 375 hamburgers!

Tigers have the
...ipes.

Tiger

This is a snow leopard.

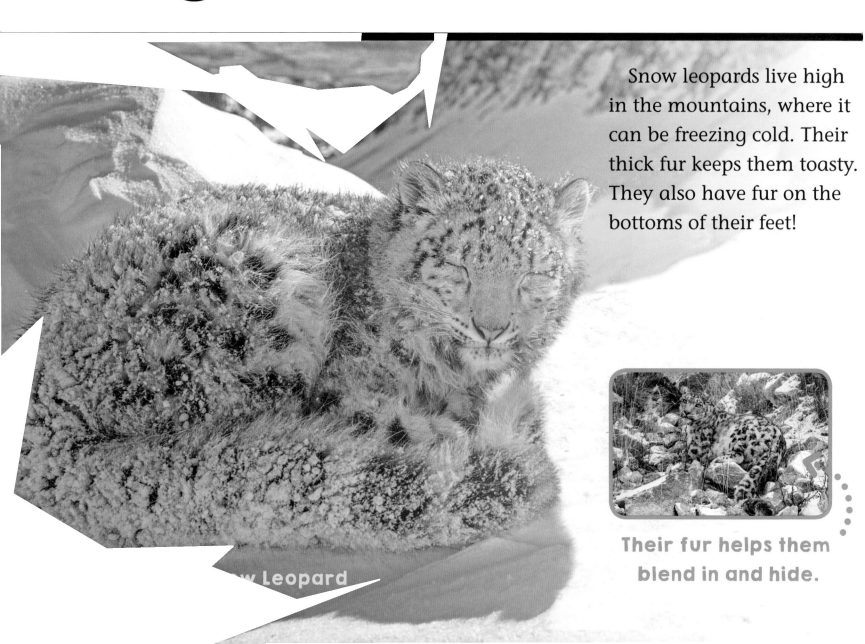

Snow leopards live high in the mountains, where it can be freezing cold. Their thick fur keeps them toasty. They also have fur on the bottoms of their feet!

Snow Leopard

Their fur helps them blend in and hide.

This is a jaguar.

Snake

Jaguar

Jaguars have one of the strongest bites of all the wild cats. A jaguar's **jaw** can even crunch through a turtle's shell! It makes biting through a snake like this easy.

This is a bobcat.

Not all wild cats are big! A bobcat is only twice the size of a pet cat. Baby bobcats are even smaller. Some people call them bobkittens!

Bobcats

Fur Fun!

Look at the fur. Can you name the wild cat it belongs to?

1

2

3

1. jaguar, 2. tiger, 3. snow leopard

Chapter 2

Wild Cats in Action

What can a wild cat do?

Cougar

This wild cat is leaping.

Cougars are great at jumping! They leap through the air to attack their **prey**. A cougar can soar 15 feet high—that's more than two basketball players tall!

long tail

Cougar

strong back legs

sharp claws

big paws

This wild cat is climbing.

Leopards are talented climbers. They use their sharp claws and strong muscles to **scale** trees. Then they surprise their prey by attacking from above.

Leopard

This wild cat is running.

Go, cheetah, go! Cheetahs are the fastest wild cats. Cheetahs **sprint** up to 70 miles per hour. That's faster than most cars go on highways!

Cheetah

This wild cat is swimming.

Some wild cats do not like going in the water, but tigers do! They are super swimmers. They sometimes swim to cool off when they are hot.

Tiger

Lions roar to show their strength. A special part of their throat lets them make this booming sound. A lion's roar is almost as loud as an ambulance siren!

Lion

ROAR!

16

Chapter 3

The Cub Club

A baby lion is called a cub. Its pride takes care of it.

Lion Cub

This cub is being carried.

Lionesses take care of their cubs. A lioness will use her mouth to carefully carry her cubs and hide them in bushes.

Lioness and Cub

18

This cub is being licked.

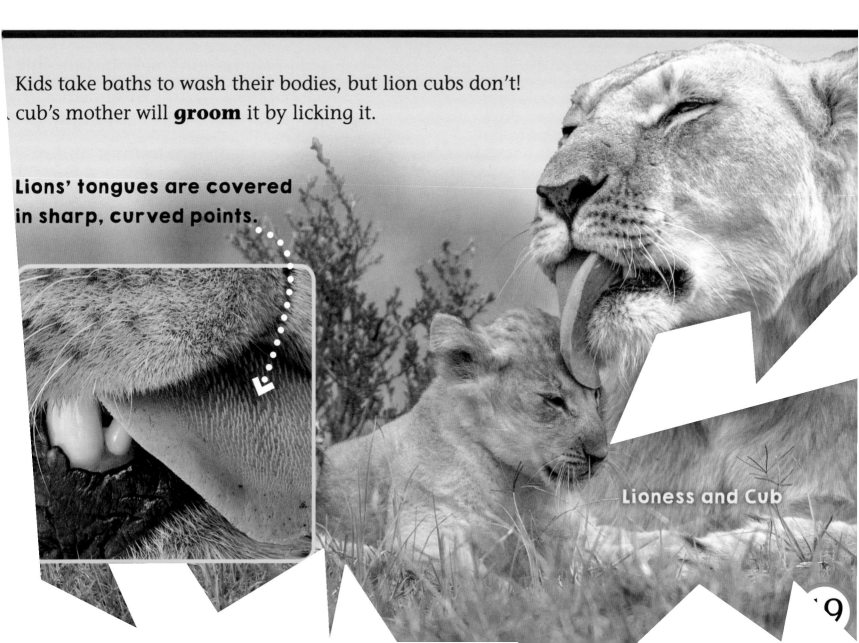

Kids take baths to wash their bodies, but lion cubs don't! cub's mother will **groom** it by licking it.

Lions' tongues are covered in sharp, curved points.

Lioness and Cub

9

This cub is playing.

Lion cubs don't play just for fun. They play to learn! By chasing, jumping, wrestling, and climbing, they are learning to hunt and protect themselves.

Young cubs ha

This cub is learning to roar.

SQUEAK!

Lion cubs can't roar right away. They must practice! In the beginning, their roars sound more like squeaks. With time, they will sound as loud as their parents!

Lion Cubs

Glossary

carnivores: (**kahr**-nuh-vorz)
Animals that eat meat

jaw:
(jaw) The bones that make up an animal's mouth

jaw

groom: (groom)
To brush and clean

mane:
(mayn)
The long, bushy fur around a male lion's head and neck

prey: (pray) An animal that is hunted for food by another animal

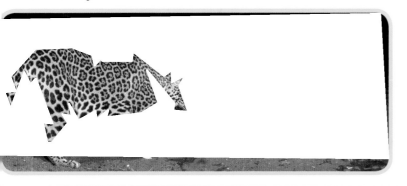

scale: (skayl) To climb

sprint: (sprint) To run fast over a short distance

pride: (pride) A family of lions

Index

Photos ©: cover: Burrard-Lucas/Nature Picture Library; cover face icons and throughout: Giuseppe_R/Shutterstock; back cover: Sergey Gorshkov/Minden Pictures; 3: GlobalP/iStockphoto; 4 left: Kantapatp/iStockphoto; 4 center: GlobalP/iStockphoto; 4 right: Joel Sartore/Getty Images; 4-5 background: Suriyawut_Khongyuen/Shutterstock; 5 center: clarst5/Shutterstock; 5 right: Barrett Hedges, Getty Images; 6: Edward Myles/Minden Pictures; 7 main: Andyworks/iStockphoto; 7 inset: anankkml/iStockphoto; 8 main: Andy Rouse/Minden Pictures; 8 inset: Sebastian Kennerknecht/Minden Pictures; 9: Chris Brunskill Ltd/Getty Images; 10 main: Tim Fitzharris/Minden Pictures; 10 inset top: Joel Sartore/Getty Images; 10 inset center: anankkml/iStockphoto; 10 inset bottom: clarst5/Shutterstock; 11: Illg, Gordon & Cathy/Animals Animals; 12: Mc Donald Wildlife Photog/Animals Animals; 13: Sergey Gorshkov/Minden Pictures; 14 main: Gérard Lacz/Biosphoto; 14 inset: Elliott Neep/Minden Pictures; 15: Juniors Bildarchiv GmbH/Alamy Images; 16: Shin Yoshino/Minden Pictures; 17: Beverly Joubert/National Geographic Creative; 18: Maggy Meyer/Shutterstock; 19 main: Anup Shah/Getty Images; 19 inset: Art Wolfe/Danita Delimont Stock Photography; 20: Suzi Eszterhas/Minden Pictures; 21: Manoj Shah/Getty Images; 22 top left: Andyworks/iStockphoto; 22 top right: Ben Landy/iStockphoto; 22 bottom left: Anup Shah/Getty Images; 22 bottom right: GlobalP/iStockphoto; 23 top left: GlobalP/iStockphoto; 23 top right: Winfried Wisniewski/Minden Pictures; 23 bottom left: Sebastian Kennerknecht/Minden Pictures; 23 bottom right: Auscape/UIG/Getty Images.

Library of Congress Cataloging-in-Publication Data
Names: Silverstein, Rebecca, author.
Title: The wild cats book / by Rebecca Silverstein.
Description: New York, NY: Children's Press®, an imprint of Scholastic Inc.,
2020. | Series: Side by side | Includes index.
Identifiers: LCCN 2019004845| ISBN 9780531238431 (library binding) | ISBN
9780531246603 (paperback)
Subjects: LCSH: Wildcat--Juvenile literature.
Classification: LCC QL737.C23 S554 2020 | DDC 599.75/26--dc23

Brought to you by the editors of *Let's Find Out*®. Original Design by Sandy Mayer, Joan Michael and Judith E. Christ for Scholastic Inc.

1 2 3 4 5 6 7 8 9 10 R 29 28 27 26 25 24 23 22 21 20